Living in the
Amazon Rainforest

Anita Ganeri

www.raintreepublishers.co.uk
Visit our website to find out more information about **Raintree** books.

To order:
☎ Phone 44 (0) 1865 888112
🖹 Send a fax to 44 (0) 1865 314091
🖥 Visit the Raintree bookshop at **www.raintreepublishers.co.uk** to browse our catalogue and order online.

First published in Great Britain by Raintree, Halley Court, Jordan Hill, Oxford OX2 8EJ, part of Pearson Education. Raintree is a registered trademark of Pearson Education Ltd.

© Pearson Education Ltd 2008
First published in paperback in 2009
The moral right of the proprietor has been asserted.

Editorial: Catherine Veitch
Design: Richard Parker and Manhattan Design
Illustration: International Mapping
Picture Research: Hannah Taylor and Maria Joannou
Production: Alison Parsons

Originated by Modern Age
Printed and bound in China by CTPS

ISBN 978-1 4062 0826 9 (hardback)
12 11 10 09 08
10 9 8 7 6 5 4 3 2 1

ISBN 978-1 4062 0836 8 (paperback)
12 11 10 09 08
10 9 8 7 6 5 4 3 2 1

British Library Cataloguing in Publication Data
Ganeri, Anita, 1961-
Living in the Amazon rainforest. - (World cultures)
981.1'3

A full catalogue record for this book is available from the British Library.

Acknowledgements
The publishers would like to thank the following for permission to reproduce photographs: Alamy Images pp. **16** (Sue Cunningham Photographic), **29** (James Quine); Art Directors and Trip/ Bob Masters pp. **9, 14, 15, 21**; Corbis pp. **20** (Owen Franken), **22** (Tom Brakefield), **25** (Sygma), **28** (Royalty Free); Digital Vision pp. **7, 18**; FLPA/ Tui De Roy/ Minden Pictures p. **6**; Getty Images/ Time Life Pictures p. **13**; Getty Images (Victor Englebert/ Time & Life Pictures) pp. **4, 8, 19, 23**; NHPA pp. **17** (Martin Harvey), **12** (Ross Nolly); Panos Pictures/ Jerry Callow p. **24**; Rex Features pp. **10** (Action Press), **27** (Sipa Press); Still Pictures/ Mark Edwards pp. **11, 26**.

Cover photograph of a Yanomami man in Brazil made up for a feast, reproduced with permission of Robert Harding/ Robin Tenison.

Every effort has been made to contact copyright holders of any material reproduced in this book. Any omissions will be rectified in subsequent printings if notice is given to the publishers.

Contents

Some words are printed in bold, **like this**. You can find out what they mean on page 31.

The Yanomami

The Yanomami are a group of people who live in South America. The name "Yanomami" means "human being". There are over 20,000 Yanomami. About half of the Yanomami population live in the country of Brazil. The other half live in Venezuela (see map on page 5). The Yanomami live in thick, green **rainforest**.

◀ A group of Yanomami men shelter from the rain underneath a banana leaf in the Amazon rainforest.

The Yanomami live in the Amazon rainforest. This is the biggest rainforest in the world. The huge Amazon River runs through it. The rainforest covers an area of about 6 million square kilometres (2.3 million square miles). It is almost the size of Australia.

The first Yanomami

The Yanomami have lived in the rainforest for thousands of years. Long ago, the first Yanomami travelled from Asia to North America (see smaller map below). Then they headed south to South America. Gradually, they moved closer and closer to the River Amazon.

▲ This map shows where the Yanomami live in the Amazon rainforest. Their lands are split between the countries of Brazil and Venezuela.

Life in the forest

The Yanomami live deep inside the **rainforest**. They call the rainforest *Urihi*. Urihi means "forest land". Everything they need comes from the rainforest.

◄ Rainwater collects in the cup-shaped leaves of plants called bromeliads. It is good to drink.

RAINFOREST CLIMATE

The **equator** runs through the Amazon rainforest. The equator is an imaginary line around the Earth. The **climate** is always hot and steamy. In the wet season, it rains heavily on most days. It rains less in the dry season, but it can still be very wet. The heat and damp are ideal conditions for plants to grow all year round.

Survival skills

The Yanomami have learned special skills for surviving. They know which rainforest plants are good for food and medicine. They know which plants are good for building materials. They know which rainforest animals to hunt for food. The Yanomami share the forest with the plants and animals. They treat it with great care and respect.

▸ A brightly coloured bird called a toucan, perches on the branch of a rainforest tree. Yanomami children sometimes keep toucans as pets.

Life in the community

The Yanomami live in hundreds of small villages. These are scattered widely across the **rainforest**. Between 40 and 150 people live in each village.

Everyone in the village has a job. Some people help to build houses or go hunting. Others grow fruit and vegetables. Today, some villagers trade with people from other **cultures**. They give the Yanomami factory-made goods, such as metal cooking pots or wrist-watches.

◀ Yanomami women carry baskets of manioc (see page 15) which they have been to gather in the forest.

▲ A Yanomami chief from Venezuela carries a bow and arrows for hunting.

Village visiting

Each village has a leader, or chief. The chief looks after the village. He is in charge of activities, such as building a new house. Other villagers can come to the chief for advice. The Yanomami regularly travel through the forest to other villages. They visit friends and relatives. They also attend feasts and other celebrations.

YANOMAMI LANGUAGES

The Yanomami speak different languages, depending on where they live. The languages are quite similar. People often understand each other even when their language is slightly different. Here are some words and phrases to try out:

Awe	(Aw-eh)	Yes
Ma	(Mah)	No
Ara	(Ah-rah)	Macaw (large parrot)
Waka	(Wah-kah)	Armadillo (mammal)
Iro	(Ee-roh)	Howler monkeys
Oshe	(Osh-eh)	Termites (insects)

A Yanomami house

In many Yanomami villages, everyone lives together in one big, round hut. The hut is called a *yano*. There is a large open space in the middle of the *yano*. This is where Yanomami children play. Feasts and dances are held here as well.

A traditional *yano* is made with materials from the **rainforest**. The walls are made from tree trunks. The tree trunks are tied together with long, rope-like **vines**. The roof is made from palm leaves. Today, some of the Yanomami build modern, square huts. They use factory-made materials given to them by outsiders who come to the forest.

◀ Many Yanomami families live together in a round hut called a *yano*.

Inside the yano

More than 20 families may live inside the *yano*. Each family has its own space. Families sleep in **hammocks**, hung up around a fire. The fire is used for cooking and heating. Each family hangs its baskets, containers, and tools from the *yano*'s roof.

◄ In the *yano*, hammocks are strung up one above the other, with the youngest children sleeping at the bottom.

MOVING HOUSE

Every few years, the *yano* becomes leaky and full of insects. The villagers move out of the old *yano*. They clear another space in the forest. They build a new *yano* and burn down the old house.

Daily life

In a Yanomami village, men and women traditionally do different jobs. The men hunt animals for food. The women look after the children and do the cooking, as well as collect water from the river and firewood from the forest. Both men and women work on the village gardens.

▸ A garden is cut out of the forest. Pumpkins, sweet potatoes, and cassava (plants with roots that can be eaten) are growing.

▼ A Yanomami man in the village garden digs up some manioc (see page 15) with a knife.

Gardening

Every village has its own "garden". This is a clearing in the forest where people grow crops, such as **plantains** (a type of banana). They also grow sugarcane and sweet potatoes. The women clear away weeds and plant new crops. They collect cotton, which they use to make **hammocks** and clothing.

FAMILY LIFE

A Yanomami family may be made up of a father, mother, and several children. The Yanomami do not have a special **ceremony** when they get married. They simply hang their hammocks next to each other in the *yano*. For the first few years, mothers keep their babies with them while they work. Children sleep with their mother in her hammock until they are about five years old or until a new baby is born into the family.

13

Yanomami food

Traditionally, the Yanomami get all the food they need from the **rainforest**. They eat rainforest plants. They hunt rainforest animals for meat. Today, some Yanomami also eat Western food, such as tinned food.

▲ A Yanomami man cuts up a fish that he has caught in the river.

MANIOC BREAD

Manioc is a vegetable. It looks like a long potato. If it is not prepared properly, it can be poisonous. Manioc is a very important part of the Yanomami diet. It is made into bread. The manioc is peeled and grated. The poisonous juice is squeezed out. The paste that is left is made into thick, flat cakes. These are left in the sun to dry. Then the cakes are baked over the fire.

▸ A Yanomami woman grates manioc, which she will make into bread.

Traditional food

The Yanomami grow a wide range of fruit and vegetables in their gardens. **Plantains** are eaten at many meals. They are boiled or roasted. Sometimes they are mashed up with water to make a drink. The Yanomami also collect many plants that grow wild in the forest including peach palm fruits. They also collect Brazil nuts, pineapples, and avocados. Fish are caught in the river, using baskets or poisoned arrows.

Going hunting

The Yanomami hunt **rainforest** animals, such as **tapirs** (see opposite), for their meat. Tapirs are large, pig-like animals. The Yanomami also hunt monkeys, giant anteaters, and wild pigs. It is very important for Yanomami men to be good hunters. They earn respect by bringing back meat for their families.

A hunt sets off

The hunters leave the village early in the morning. They walk through the forest, following animal **tracks**. They have to be skilful. Many rainforest animals hide away in the daytime. The hunters use whistles and hand signals to speak to each other. They do not want to scare away the animals.

▶ This Yanomami boy is practising with his bow and arrow to become a good hunter.

▲ Tapirs, like this one, are hunted by the Yanomami for their meat.

BEING A HUNTER

The hunters never say the names of the animals they hunt. They believe that it will make the animals disappear. Instead, they may call the animal they hunt a "warrior". Traditionally, they kill the animals with bows and arrows. The arrows are dipped in poison made from the bark of a rainforest tree. Nowadays, they also use shotguns. Back in the **yano**, the hunters share out the meat with the other families. Hunters never eat meat from animals that they have killed themselves.

Clothes and dressing up

The weather is warm and sticky in the **rainforest**. The Yanomami do not need to wear many clothes. Traditionally, both men and women are naked or wear cotton **loincloths**. Loincloths look like short aprons. Today, some Yanomami also wear Western-style clothes, such as T-shirts. They might also wear shorts and dresses. They get these clothes from outsiders.

▸ Red feathers from a macaw are believed to have strong magical powers.

Dressing up

Yanomami men and women like to wear jewellery. The jewellery is made from forest materials. They make necklaces from strings of seeds or animal teeth. They pierce their ears and wear flowers or feathers as earrings. They also pierce their noses and lower lips. They put short, thin sticks through the holes.

BODY PAINTING

The Yanomami like to paint their faces and bodies for feasts and other celebrations. They use red and black patterns. These patterns are based on rainforest plants and animals. The red and black paints are made from crushed seeds. The paint can also be made from the fruits of rainforest trees.

On special occasions, men like to wear feather headdresses and armbands. The feathers come from rainforest birds, such as macaws. They might also get feathers from parrots and toucans. The Yanomami believe that the feathers give them special powers and protect them from evil **spirits**.

◄ A Yanomami man has painted his face and body, and put on a feather armband ready for a special occasion.

Learning and leisure

Today, some Yanomami children go to schools run by the government. But most children do not go to school. Instead, they learn useful skills from their parents. They soon know which animals to hunt. They quickly learn which plants to use for food and medicine. They learn about Yanomami history and beliefs by listening to stories.

▲ Yanomami children are taught in an outdoor school in the Amazon **rainforest**.

Growing up

Yanomami boys practise their hunting skills using miniature bows and arrows. They hunt small animals, such as lizards. They also hunt frogs and birds. They spend most of the day with their friends, climbing trees and swimming in the river. Girls have less time to play. From an early age, they learn how to cook and make **hammocks**. They also help to look after the younger children.

▶ These Yanomami children are learning how to get honey from a bees' nest inside a rainforest tree.

THE STORY OF FIRE

A Yanomami **legend,** or story, says that long ago, the Yanomami did not have fire to cook on. They ate raw food. Then, lightning struck the forest and started a fire. Iwariwa, the **cayman**, swallowed the fire. He kept it inside his body. One day, someone tricked Iwariwa into laughing. He opened his mouth and the fire escaped. That is how the Yanomami discovered fire.

21

Yanomami beliefs

The Yanomami believe that all living things have powerful **spirits**. The spirits live in *yanos* in the sky. The spirits often come down to Earth. They can be helpful or harmful. They can cure people who are ill. They can help hunters to find animals. They can also cause sickness and bring bad luck.

▸ The Yanomami believe that every **rainforest** animal has a spirit. The most powerful spirit is that of the jaguar.

◄ When a shaman talks to an animal spirit, he acts like that animal. He uses animal noises and movements.

Talking to the spirits

The Yanomami believe that **shamans** are the only people who can talk to the spirits. When someone is ill, the shaman calls to the spirits. They ask the spirit to visit and help the person. Different spirits have different powers.

YANOMAMI UNIVERSE

The Yanomami believe that the **universe** has four layers. Nothing lives in the top layer. This is where the universe began. The next layer down is a beautiful place in the sky. This is where the spirits of dead people go. Below this is the layer containing Earth. The bottom layer is a terrible place. It is where the spirits of people go if they fall from the sky layer.

Ceremonies and dances

Sometimes the Yanomami invite guests from other villages for a special feast. The space in the middle of the *yano* is cleared for singing and dancing. The women prepare special food. They boil **plantains** and roast meat. Everyone gets dressed up.

◀ Yanomami dancers perform at a feast. Some dances may last for many hours.

Funeral ceremony

A *yaimo* is held when someone dies. This is a special **ceremony**. A *yaimo* may last for several days. The ceremony begins with singing and dancing. There is plenty to eat and drink. An important part of a *yaimo* is trading with people from other villages. Traditionally, the Yanomami do not use money. They **exchange** (swap) goods instead. They might trade an axe and some fish hooks, for a new bow and arrow.

▸ These Yanomami are dressed in special costumes ready to go to a funeral feast.

A FUNERAL CUSTOM

When a Yanomami dies, his or her body is burned on a fire. The ashes are collected and put into hollowed-out **gourds**. At the *yaimo*, the **shaman** mixes the ashes with banana juice. The dead person's family drink the mixture. The Yanomami believe that the dead person's **spirit** will live on in his or her family.

Under threat

The Yanomami have lived in the **rainforest** for thousands of years. They have learned how to use the forest without harming it. But today, the forest is being destroyed. This is harming the plants and animals, which the Yanomami rely on for food.

▲ These rainforest trees are being cut down and burned to make space for a cattle ranch (large farm).

YANOMAMI LAND

Many people have tried to help the Yanomami. In 1992, the government of Brazil set aside part of the forest. They called it "Yanomami Park". This was for the Yanomami only and it was somewhere they could live safely. Sadly, some gold miners are still breaking the rules and going in the park.

▶ Gold miners look for gold in the Amazon rainforest. Digging mines, like this one, is damaging the forest.

Yanomami in danger

Some rainforest **products** are very valuable. In the 1980s, gold was discovered on Yanomami land. This was in Brazil (see map on page 5). Thousands of miners came to the rainforest to dig up the gold and sell it. The miners shot many animals. They poisoned the rivers with **chemicals**. They built roads and damaged huge areas of forest. Many Yanomami were shot. Thousands more Yanomami died from diseases, such as flu and measles. They caught these illnesses from the gold miners.

Could you be a Yanomami?

Try this quiz. Could you live in the **rainforest** like the Yanomami?

1. What does the name "Yanomami" mean?
A) Human being B) Little person C) Tall people

2. Which huge river runs through the Amazon rainforest?
A) Mississippi B) Amazon C) Nile

3. What do the Yanomami call the rainforest?
A) **Yano** B) *Urihi* C) *Nano*

4. Which rainforest plants would you get water from?
A) Bromeliad B) **Vine** C) Water lily

5. What do the Yanomami live in?
A) Tent B) Castle C) *Yano*

6. Which crop might you find in a Yanomami's garden?
A) **Plantain** B) Potatoes C) Rice

7. Which animals do the Yanomami hunt?
A) Cow B) **Tapir** C) Dinosaurs

8. Which bird's red feathers are very special?
A) A macaw's B) A sparrow's C) A hummingbird's

9. Which animal might you meet in the Amazon rainforest?
A) Giraffe B) Jaguar C) Polar bear

10. Whom do the Yanomami go to when they are sick?
A) **Shaman** B) Friend C) Nurse

Find out for yourself

Books to read

Horrible Geography: Bloomin' Rainforests, Anita Ganeri
    (Scholastic Children's Books, 2001)
Rainforest People, Edward Parker (Hodder Wayland, 2002)
The Vanishing Rainforest, Richard Platt (Frances Lincoln, 2003)

Websites

www.survival-international.org
The website of Survival International, an organisation that helps threatened people around the world to protect their way of life.

www.ran.org
The Rainforest Action Network's website. RAN works to save the rainforests and protect the lives of rainforest people.

www.rainforestfoundationuk.org
Fascinating facts about the rainforest and the people that live in them.

www.socioambiental.org
A detailed guide to the rainforest people of Brazil.
English version available.

Glossary

cayman animal related to alligators and crocodiles

ceremony public celebration

chemical strong substance used in making and cleaning things

climate type of weather a place has over a long time

culture groups of people with a particular way of life

equator imaginary line around the Earth. The places along the equator have hot weather all year round.

exchange swap something for something else

gourd fruit with a hard shell. When the fruit is taken out, the shells are dried and used as drinking cups and containers.

hammock long piece of cotton cloth, which is hung up by both ends and used as a bed

legend ancient, traditional story

loincloth short piece of cloth that is worn around a person's waist

plantain banana-like fruit

product object that is made or grown

rainforest thick, green forest that grows around the equator

shaman person who communicates with the spirit world and calls on the spirits to heal sick people

spirit invisible force inside people and other living things

tapir large, pig-like animal that lives in the rainforest

track footprint or mark left by an animal in the rainforest soil

universe another name for the world and everything around it

vine long, woody root of a rainforest plant, which grows high up on the tree branches

yaimo Yanomami funeral ceremony

yano round hut where many Yanomami families live together

Index